CRUSH

Crush

will stockton / d. gilson

punctum books ∗ brooklyn, ny

CRUSH
© Will Stockton & D. Gilson, 2014.

First published in 2014 by
punctum books
Brooklyn, New York
http://punctumbooks.com

ISBN-13: 978-0615978956
ISBN-10: 0615978959

Library of Congress Cataloging Data is available from the Library of Congress.

Cover and Interior Images: photography by Caleb Suttles.

Facing-page drawing by Heather Masciandaro.

Table of Contents

PART III: IN THE GARDEN, OR BEFORE THE FALL

It's pretty obvious that you've got a crush.
That magic in your pants, it's making me blush.

- Ke$ha

If we could no longer enjoy an afterlife earned by our good deeds,
we could at least leave behind a sense of our achievement,
measured aesthetically, and the most beautiful art we could
practice would be the art of self-realization through
friendship. ... But perhaps I misunderstood him.

- Edmund White, *The Farewell Symphony*

Lunch with the Scholar

Because sometimes it will happen like this:
outside, yes, the steady, false start to spring.
Inside, the scholar pardons himself to piss
and you can't stop staring at the lime green
band of his underwear. What you do: blush,
       hum that line of Sonnet 87—
Farewell, thou art too dear for my possessing—
because what you know now is this: longing
knows no bounds of rationality, knows
       neither temporality nor justice.
When he returns to the table, you speak
of television and Prince, now Jehovah's
Witness. Your conversion, just like his own,
       born long ago, ignites here in a flash.

Beginning Endlessly

Sonnet 87 begins with a farewell to a lover troped as property secured by the "bonds" of law—a law that nonetheless does not determine the meaning of possession throughout the poem. To possess also means to "hold" and to "grant." A possession is a "gift," something "had … as a dream." Possession is ghostly, an inhabitation, a sudden arrest.

I met you at lunch. Later that night, amidst a crush of men in a steam room, I watched you fuck someone several inches taller than you, standing on your tiptoes to slam yourself into him for me. I couldn't touch you; those are the rules of possession to which I have agreed. But physical touch is only one mode of contact, one way of having.

In class, my explanation of Shakespeare's sonnets goes something like this:

In a world both fallen and in free-fall, where Beauty and Poetry stand against Time and Age and Death, a man falls *hard* in love with a boy. This love is friendly and paternal and pedagogical and erotic and competitive and overbearing in ways that might make you uncomfortable but did not necessarily have the same effects on Renaissance readers. Later in the sequence, but who knows how much time has passed, the man falls in love with a woman with a love that is much more socially transgressive because it's interracial and she's not monogamous. (But what is monogamy?) The boy seems to be involved with her, too. The man then likely gets VD, likely syphilis, and ends the sequence in a medicinal bath. All throughout there are discussions of the various rules and laws, explicit and implicit, social and discursive, governing these relationships, and

4

experiments in and with the lexicons structuring desire (also called syphilis) and its experience.

I'm leaving a bunch of things out, but that's the story in sum—if it's *the* story, which it may not be because we have to ask questions, too, about order, pronouns, and the roles editors and readers play in shaping the story the sonnets tell and the sentiments they voice. Also, we need to understand something about Petrarchan conventions if we're going to understand the sonnets as pervy remodels and dis-eased iterations of those desiring machines, as queer possessions of their voice. For many of the sonnets are inappropriate by the very Petrarchan standards they cite.

In Aranye Fradenburg's words, the sonnets describe "the love you feel for inappropriate objects: for someone thirty years older, thirty years younger. The kind of love that makes a fool, a pervert, a stalker out of you."[1] Let's start here, for much of this description applies to Petrarchan conventions as well. Let's start here, with this affective entrance into the poems and the impossibility of dispossessing the other's voice in the manufacture of one's own machine. Let's start here, with a vision of poems as indexes of crushes rendered inappropriate, unhealthy by some gradation of difference and level of intensity. With the question of what distinguishes a crush from love if both turn you into a different self.

I: After the Fall

But these melancholias also show us something else, which may be of
importance for our later discussions. They show us the ego divided,
fallen into pieces, one of which rages against the second.

- Sigmund Freud, "On Narcissism"

Narcissus at the Baths

Towel-wrapped Narcissus
walks bored around the square of
open-door rooms. Caught

at last in the flash
of a glance, he crushes the
gilded, corner mirror.

Retrospective

When you are nearly a third decade,
look back one. Tell that boy to slow

down, to steal time, to learn Spanish
and not French. Or to learn French

better. To visit France. Tell him brother
never means the things he says, not

faggot, not *I promise*. Go to Seattle,
live on a houseboat, study anthropology.

Study yourself in the rising tides
of the Puget Sound and soon become

a seal upon a rock washed clear of moss,
but not clean. Clean yourself. Prepare.

Move east. Love a man though you always
thought it'd be a woman. Let the man kick

your stomach, eat it raw. Leave his highway
behind on a yellow bicycle. Eat Doritos,

an entire bag, and make penance.
Move west again. Or halfway and south.

To Mexico. This is why you should
have learned Spanish in the first place.

Disappearing Act

Outside the window of my office
in this house we bought eight months ago,
a thin squirrel hops through grass
taller than he is, his brown body visible
only in swift gusts between green blades.
Despite the aftershock of winter's cold,
I need to cut the grass. But yesterday I ran
errands while you graded papers.
Later, I slipped into bed three hours after
you had fallen asleep.

Two-and-a-half years ago we sat together
on the couch in my uncle's hospital suite,
babysitting while my aunt took an evening away
from what had become the daily routine of dying.
But my uncle was not a baby. He was a body,
emaciated, swollen, carefully propped on pillows.
When he could walk, he would disappear for days,
leaving his wife and three sons at home.
And I thought this will be us, the disappearing

act yours. Here is the truth: some mornings,
I miss my boy. Drawing off his yellow tank top,
running my hands up his back, pulling
his thin frame into me, the candy on his breath.

Revelation

I gave you a bicycle because the first time
you made me a brown sugar latte I knew
it would be near impossible not to and this
seems irrational now, obsessive, but I dreamt
last night of us by the fire, me the Christ, you
John, the beloved. As I stroked your head,
you sang *Sweet Caroline* in my ear, the smell
of sandalwood on your lips as we began
to kiss, then were engulfed in flame. I awake,
startled to be having this dream again, afraid
of what the soul is trying so hard to reveal.
You will pull espresso all morning and I will
teach, meet you at Starbucks later so we can
ride bikes to the creek, strip there and swim
at a place cool and secret, ours, where no fire
can take us, though I too often wish it would.

Born Again

Deleuze says he takes philosophers from behind, giving them a child that is theirs, yet monstrous.[2] That's how one should answer any question concerning the reason one studies the past. Only the past should be pitching, and you catching, and the versions of yourself that this buggery produces—monsters of queer self-invention.

~

This is the story of how I became a born-again early modernist.

~

My boy: I drove by his house after church on a clammy Sunday, wondering whether I should knock on the door, and what I would say, and whether his mother would answer, and what I would say *then*, and whether they would be at church, too. We had met at church, and although I now attended a different one, a more liberal one—meaning that they didn't expect you to dress up, and they occasionally sang secular songs like Mike and the Mechanics' "The Living Years"—church, as institution and discourse, oriented us, or at least me. I wondered if he was still so oriented.

These wonders produced no action. I returned to my apartment to spin *what ifs*, to stalk the answer to the question I kept asking: whether there was any hope of reconstituting as friendship, as *philia*, a bond that had suffered the confession of sexual desire; of restructuring our friendship in a way that both excluded *eros*—if that was what I wanted, which I did not—and allowed me to continue desiring, in proximity, and possessing.

On the day of my drive-by, I was trying not to be gay. The moniker was one I had adopted six months previously only to seek salvation from it, much like I sought salvation from its synonym *sinner*. I stranded myself between identities and in time, an *ex-gay*, defined myself by my refusal of a former self who would nonetheless not seal himself in the past. In a windowless office on the ground floor of an artless brick building, my counselor would tell me that God did not make people gay; that homosexuality was the result of a perversion in the divinely sanctioned trajectory of desire; and that this perversion was the result of improper bonding with my parents, especially by father, whom we blamed for a distance he did not occupy. Of course I had been "turned on" by men, my counselor explained, because my desire, like a Freudian libidinal current, had been turned. And it could be turned back again.

But also because "friction is friction." The tautology was foundational to the fiction we were building. In this fiction, a homoerotic "turn on," a perverse swerve in the open current, only began with and stayed to linger after the friction of fallen flesh on fallen flesh. Energy was memory. Desire didn't look toward the future, but only toward the past, toward what had been, what had happened; or it used what had happened as a template for what could be. Desire had no imagination. The tautology further implied that hetero-friction would be as pleasurable to me as homo-friction had been—and maybe even more so, as heterosexual relationships are driven by the energy generated in the friction of sexual difference.

To experience friction with a woman, however, the friction God meant for me to experience in the bonds of marriage, I first had to straighten out my relationship with Jesus, the man with whom I was insufficiently intimate. Jesus, Friend and Father, needed to come closer. He needed to possess me in ways I had previously forbade him.

$\sim$

Looking back on conversion therapy now, I find its methods and its rhetoric both anachronistic and perverse. Pastoralism with a clinical veneer, conversion therapy perpetuates a pre-modern worldview in which anyone is liable to commit sinful sexual acts, to slip up sexually. Everyone is a potential sodomite.

Romans 3:23: *For all have sinned and fallen short of the glory of God.*

Or, as Osgood says at the end of *Some Like it Hot*, "Nobody's perfect."

Or as Orsino says at the end of Shakespeare's play that helped turned me gay again in college—a play that Stephen Greenblatt famously reads as a fiction that embodies the friction of sexual difference—"Cesario, come — /For so you shall be while you are a man."[3]

Yet to claim that conversion therapy has not caught up with modernity—and in doing so ceased to be—would overlook the modern species of the heterosexual occupying its foundation. Posited as the *only* sexual orientation, heterosexuality stubbornly refuses to have a history, to admit an origin outside of God and the queer eroticism of its divine guarantee. "Jesus was my first boyfriend," Michael Warner writes in his own "Memoirs of a Pentecostal Boyhood." "He loved me, personally, and told me that I was his own."[4] I claimed similar things, with no consciousness of connotation, although I do believe now in the unconscious. ("Jesus came inside me and filled me with his love." The locution is slightly off. Don't I mean He came into my heart?) If pressed, I would have stated that this love was *agape*: absolute and unconditional. It was love beyond the love of friends and parents and lovers. But the single word *love* kept it tethered to *eros*, all the more so when Christ's love was prescribed as a cure for my perversion.

Christian love, divine intimacy, and conversion therapy: the contemporary queerness of each instances what Jonathan Dollimore calls the paradox of perversity — the location of perversion within a norm rather than outside it.[5] Perversion outs itself as the friction inside the fiction. It's the insistence of the letter R in *Romeo and Juliet*, the "open arse" that suddenly redirects the current of Romeo's desire for Rosaline.[6] It's the crush of the letter that outs the fiction as the structure of internal frictions. And it's the consonance that prompts this protest from an ex-gay *cum* early modernist who spent two years of his life making few friends and no lovers. Whose epistemological contortions for the sake of love turned him into a lonely stalker. For all the dangers of conversion therapy, the worst—if I dare quantify—may be its devastation of *philia*, its denial of friendship any semblance of the erotic.

Roundtable

or, The Miltonist asks The Poets, "Why do you write poetry?"

G. Snyder speaks softly—
What use, Milton, a silly story
of our lost general parents
                    eaters of fruit?

F. O'Hara interrupts—
Now, come on, I don't believe in god, so I don't have to make
    elaborately sounded structures.

G. Brooks swirls her drink—
Mary is
a rose in a whiskey glass

M. Magdalene tugs on the sleeve of the Miltonist—
Tell me you want me to worship your feet. Tell me.

S.G. Friend rolls his eyes—
You're a stupid bitch.

F. Howe looks to heaven—
I left my body to look for one
whose image nestles in the center of a wide valley

L.E. Beale, in solidarity, twirls a baton—
If you can't get a man to marry you, you might as well be dead.

T. Williams brushes F. O'Hara's arm—
No, now seriously, putting joking aside.
Why didn't you tell me, why didn't you write me, honey,
why didn't you let me know.

F. O'Hara leaves the roundtable in tears—

K. Ryan makes eye contact with the Miltonist—
apples. As though
one had a way to climb
out of the damage
and apology.

A. Rich, cutting off K. Ryan, thank god—
My swirling wants. Your frozen lips.
The grammar turned and attacked me.

Y. Komunyakaa, visibly annoyed—
Someone lightly brushed the penis
alive.

R. Paul through a blaze of AquaNet—
Don't fuck it up.

E. Bishop lifts up her sunglasses—
the art of losing's not too hard to master
though it may look like (*Write* it!) like disaster.

D. Gilson picks at a hangnail—
Tell that boy to slow down, to steal
time, to learn Spanish and not French.

M. King tilts his head, sighs—
It would be fatal for the nation to overlook the urgency of the
    moment.

A. Ginsberg lounges now under the table, crosses his legs—
yacketayakking, screaming, vomiting, whispering facts

J. Merrill, who has never taken his eyes off the Miltonist—
Who needs it! Let the soul hang out
At Benetton—stone-washed, one size fits all.

G. Snyder, D. Gilson, L.E. Beale, in unison—
Amen. Forever and ever. Amen.

Rawr

or, Narcissus Spends the Summer Texting Matt

In June we move to separate states.

The rapture happened and I have been sent to hell.
(the phone rings, an anomaly)
You broke our text-only rule. What if my husband answered?
If he answered I would have phone sex with him.
Alas, he does not have phone sex.
When I was twelve my church made the fantastic mistake
of hiring me to do the gardening. But it was more fun to hide
in the bushes and masturbate. And there was a statue of Mary
in the garden where nothing ever got gardened.
I am losing our photo contest!
Send something obscene for my fragile mind?
No, lest I end up like Anthony Weiner.
Your husband has made you paranoid.
That's why I don't have pictures of your testicles on my phone.

In July we play Words with Friends.

Wake up and play Words with me, sex monkey.
I thought I was sex kitten.
You work in a cigarette factory now?
I'm watching fireworks from the roof of my chemical compound.

Did I mention that I sleepwalked last night?
I went to bed wearing earplugs, and this morning
those earplugs were on the counter
in the downstairs bathroom.
That wouldn't happen if you were being spooned.
> *I could have broken free.*
>> Maybe you need a leash.
> I have a hand of only vowels.
I have a dildo wand.
Do you ever want to not play Words?
LOL we don't have to play.
Light, medium, or heavy crush?
Drunk. On a farm. Sheep shitting outside
my car window. Like ya do. So nice to be home.

In August we prepare for winter.

Are you breaking up with me?
Would you miss my small penis
and pervy thoughts terribly?
I'm afraid I'd have to stalk you.
You can always come back
and be my lawn boy, remember.
America I'm putting my queer shoulder to the wheel.
That's not the song, Ginsberg.
Since you're going to Canada,
and I'll never see you again, you should
send me a cock pic.
Sorry, love. Cock pics are reserved
(the angel descends nearly, the end is nigh,
the great separation to come, an end of days)
for people I've been inside.
He wanted me to come first.
I like to jerk myself off when I'm being fucked.

My ass clenched down so hard it hurt his dick.
I scooped up some of my cum and stuck it inside his lower lip.
I knew you were the wrong fucking person to tell.
Today is your last day in America, no?
Our texts make up a 104 page document, single spaced.   .
I do not like you very much.
I love you! *What is love?* Almost there.
Cannot wait to get out of this car.

Sex Education

Take a gym period.
Segregate boys and girls.
>Girls should not be in the room
>when boys learn about the vagina.
>And boys should not be in the room
>when girls learn about the penis.
>Students feel more comfortable when
>segregated.

Provide students with a handout of Bible verses.
>1 Thessalonians 4:3-4, *It is God's will*
>*that you should be sanctified:*
>*that you should avoid sexual immorality;*
>*that each of you should learn to control*
>*your own body in a way that is holy*
>*and honorable.*

Show students slides of diseased, unholy genitals.
Compare sex to sharing a toothbrush.
Allow Dr. Dobson to instruct:
They move around,
>*in and out,*
>>*until they both have a kind of*
>>*tingly feeling*

called an orgasm,
which lasts for a minute or two.
>*It's a very satisfying experience, which husbands*
>*and wives do regularly.*

At the start of winter,
a student trips down the last stair.
Crushes his friend into the wall.
His nose fills with the smell of sweater,
of Polo Sport-soaked wool.
His friend's peachfuzz tingles his cheek
as each turns his own face away.

Again, Dr. Dobson:
>   *Homosexuality is an abnormal desire*
>   *that reflects deep problems,*
>   *but it doesn't happen very often,*
>   *and it's unlikely to happen to you.*
So not to your students.

But sitting on the edge of the bed,
watching the White Witch seduce Edmund,
this same student will surprise himself
with fifteen seconds of burning
and fall off.

Unto Others

Because sometimes it will happen like this:
I will meet you for the first time after two years
of Facebook stalking—*the most beautiful
boy in the world, no exaggeration—*
at the Cinco de Mayo party of a mutual friend.
All drunk, we will play I can't remember what game
that strips us to our underwear. When our friends
stumble to the kitchen, we will lean over and kiss,
your thin lips wrapping around mine, your tongue
pushing mine back into my mouth and me thinking,
with no more savvy than Dan Savage,
that monogamy is hard, and not what I want.

You will spend nights with me, because sharing
a bed isn't against the rules. Luke 6:31—
*Do unto others as you would have them
do unto you.* I will rest my nose
in your armpit, in the smell of artificial apple
and sweat. We will take a walk after dinner,
after a few drinks, during which I don't stop
myself from kissing you, from running my hands
down the back of your yellow tank-top,
from pulling it up to see the triangle tattoo
on your stomach, from tracing your thin frame

and pulling you into me for everyone to see.
Because he never lets me do that, not in public
and barely in private, and you make me so giddy
with your optimism, your poverty, your insistence
that six months in Argentina made you mature,
your plain expressions of desire and bodily exigencies.
Pardon me, you will say, *I just farted for like thirty seconds.*
Back in bed, I will begin to cry when your tongue
moves lower than my chest, when you roll me over
onto my stomach.

When I tell him that I need a few days,
because I'm thinking about ending us,
I will curl like a roly poly on the bed.
You will wrap yourself around me,
tell me I will always love him,
and I will know I am crushing you.
For you I will keep drinking.
For you I will rip off a cabinet door.
For you I will make miso soup that you will have to clean up.
For you I will show up at strangers' apartments
at 2:00 in the morning, kiss you in front of your friends,
lay down on stained pillows with your mouth on my neck.
For you I will tell myself that I am inventing a new way of life.
You will tell me that no other boy has been so open.
I will tell you that I am treating you the same way
I want to be treated.

What I will not tell you
is that he and I are staying together. You will hear
through my equivocations the impossibility
of our further invention.
You will sit with me in the backseat of your van,
your head on my lap, losing me back
to the person you thought you were replacing.
And a day later you will begin dating a boy

we both know is no good for you, a boy
you don't find attractive, a boy
you tell me over our now tame texts
can't or won't open himself to you.
And I will think of Romeo
replacing Rosaline with Juliet in a night's time.

Boy

*or, quickly exhausted infatuation at The Green
Lantern's "Shirtless Boys Drink Free Thursdays"*

Someone has spilt vodka on my chest.
Isn't this how it always goes? You pull

my bare torso to your bare torso,
lick my clavicle, whisper in my ear,

You taste like cardamom. Ramzi whispers
in my other ear, *Gurl, the hottest boy*

in this room has chosen you. Don't fuck it up.
Your cock-eyed Orioles cap betrays

your doctorate in classical composition
and under this light, your skin glistens blue.

Then, I see you clearly: honey-hued,
like the new Langston Hughes portrait

at the Corcoran. *Do you like poetry?*
Your eyes blaze. You flick your tongue:

                    Call me slave boy.
And now *I look at the world*

from awakening eyes in a black face.
I know that my own pale face betrays

me. That—finally!—when I know
what the boy who's chosen me

really wants. To crave his body.
　　　　To say, *Come here, slave.*

To *look at my own body*
　　　　with eyes no longer blind.

I want to give this boy who's chosen
　　　　me all that he desires,

my talking body, my sovereign lust
　　　　pulsing under pulsing disco

lights. But I know the weight of it,
　　　　what we all want, I cannot bear.

Dakota

If I could I would rescue that boy,
not drive him home but keep him here.
Cut his hair. Take him to the dentist.
Buy him clothes that fit and stop his smoking.

I would cut his hair myself, sweep the oily strands
into my dustpan and open his pores.
Homeschool him, because eighteen is too old
for ninth grade and eighth is not enough.

I would teach him to cook. Ban Pepsi
and Cheetos and make guacamole with fresh
avocados and minced onions and lime.
He would sit to eat every night at 7:00.

I would see what makes him twitch.
His mother says, *It's hard to keep these kids
off drugs.* In which case rehab, counseling.
He can have my bed.

I will not pay him to clean my toilets,
to scrub my showers and my floors
for sixty dollars he splits with his mother
and a ride home to a house that keeps moving.

I will give him an allowance he can use to buy
DVDs. Books. Comics. Candy I have banned.
Teach him to read. How to curl his tongue
around letters, to know *i* before *e* except after *c*.

I will love this mother's son like no one will.
Keep him from harm, jail, the military.
From men who pay for more than cleaning.
From a wife who cleans my house for sixty dollars

and has nothing else to live.

For Will, The Same-Named Boy

I thought I had you when you shuffled
                              down the hall
and joined me on the bed.
               You and your rat terrier, Draco,
          who flipped onto his back and shed.
But. *No, you cuddle with Draco. When's lunch?*
When Howard gets out of the shower.
But time is a weak measure.
               Last year, I crushed
          into your boyfriend.
               Sometimes, I crush still
          because time is no
measure.
For now, I pull you into me
          and you fall,
               a tree with roots
          dug deep into the white pillows,
but not deep enough.

The Chosen

I met Benjamin in hot July outside
the yogurt shop on Forbes.

We walked and in front of his building,
he asked, *Come up*.

I knew this, no question,
and we kissed, pulled t-shirts over

heads and groped, kicked off
shoes, unbuckled belts, shoved

our jeans down and stepped
into the world.

We fell to the bed, salted
nipples and chests and obliques

with the rough of our tongues.
Our bodies glided

in the heat,
sweat everywhere, beginning

to finish. After, he slept. I thumbed
his necklace, Star of David,

whispered, *How far we fall from grace.*
How far we do not fall.

Adam Tries Again

Adam straddles the fallen trunk next to Raphael, says, "So collateral
love and dearest amite," their thighs touching, lateral

skin upon angel flesh, " so I love Eve, but I'm not loving
how you're always talking subjugation blah, blah, blah sex

makes us equal with animals blah blah blah, telling me
to butch it up, bro. I'm just out here making the best

heaven I know how with what the Father has bestowed." Raphael
contracts his brow. Adam senses Eve is about to become collateral

damage, and he hates this, knowing that Eve is, in fact, superior
to himself—sensible, handy around the garden. Nothing coextensive

about their marriage, no. Adam is, as they'd come to say,
not wearing the pants. Though no one is yet. That comes later.

.

Adam refrains, "God promised me *thy likeness, thy fit help, thy other self,* but gurl, I took what he said more literal.

Someone like, uh, you." Adam shifts his gaze to look at the angel directly, "and you know I don't mean to complain and complain,

but anytime we go to the beach, Eve is too busy staring at her own reflection that no one is there to lather

me up with coconut oil. You know how easy I burn in direct sunlight." Adam grazes Raphael's knee, lateral

to his own still, but now shaking from touch. "So, I've been wondering, what if I break up with her and we agree to just be friends, coleaders

of this collateral in God's wager with the Enemy? I don't know. I need time to think. Boys weekend in Tel Aviv? You, me, God?

Or just us is fine, too." Adam hands Raphael a slip of paper, etched with coal: his name, his number—*call me later.*

Sonnet Before Introduction to Shakespeare

In the parking lot of the community college
where I teach, a young woman walks by
a Chevy Camaro where a young man sits
listening to Eminem and smoking weed.

Though I am not old, I am too old for this
I think, walking into the gray cinderblock
building. I sit by a window in the faculty
lounge and check my e-mail. Outside

the man is talking to the woman through
the lowered glass. He turns up the bass
as Eminem sings *I'm not afraid, I'm not
afraid, to take a chance, to take a chance*,

and she kisses him through the car window
as I wish for them, love, despite what I know.

II: Falling

It is very difficult to keep the line between the past
and the present, you know what I mean?

- Little Edie Beale

Echo to Narcissus

Drunk on a porch in the sudden
        summer of Washington,
                as the blossoms
of a nearby cherry tree bloom
for the spring that promised
        but never came.
Drunk on a porch with Tony Kushner
        who's won the Pulitzer,
        a man who asks me
about my poetry,
                isn't it funny?
That the sudden spring
        that never came
                is now summer?
That the man I want to be
talking to
        is you, in fact,
        not the one before me,
the one with an Oscar nomination,
        but you,
Narcissus, in the land of the pines
        eight hours south of here,
on the map I've already etched
to memory.

Foreplay

I gush—*love this song!*—and rush to his stereo
in the corner ("Alligator" by Tegan and Sara).

I'm dancing, dressed hip, fit for the scenario
in a Flaming Lips tee, ripped, and a pair of

briefs (highlighter yellow, American Apparel).
I'm dancing in his bedroom. He laughs, shakes

the bottle of poppers from the nightstand, takes
a hit into each nostril, his eyes rage, now feral,

set ablaze. He leaps toward me, puts the bottle
to my nose. Says, *Here my boy, just breathe.*

I admit—*I'm no good at this.* I feel his heart throttle
inside his Marlboro chest. He licks his teeth

then kisses me deep. In the corner, the stereo
thrums. He hooks my waistband. It won't be long.

Fall, Then Falling

> The more flexible heterosexual body tolerates
> a certain amount of queerness.
>
> - Robert McRuer

I'm falling on the playground
of graduate school
for the boy who sits across

from me, St. Michael
of Sly Smiles in the seminar
on contemporary queer theory.

And I am a bonafide queer—
St. Michael of Skinny Jeans
tells me—*I dated men*

for ten years before this,
when I ask about
the girlfriend on his arm

in the Facebook profile
picture I've looked
at every day for the last

two, maybe three, weeks.

∼

I am always falling
for the Catholic boy
who cannot save me,

O Michael of great miracles,
O thou of goodly counsels,
O soldier, O will you wear

those gray pants to class
tonight, the ones
which make me want

to kneel before your altar
and bear you beyond
my lips, a communion

at which I pray—*look down
upon me, benevolent
boy, I beseech thee.*

Freudian slip: when Marty,
my brother, overdosed,
methamphetamines chased

with moonshine, I became
lost in the Catholic hospital
where his body awaited

the resurrection. Wandered
to the chapel. Knelt at the altar.
Prayed to that Christ,

a rush of blood to my groin.

~

At a tiny apartment party
I sweat. I sweat and lean hard
against a white tile counter,

watch you across the winding map
of dining nook and living room,
where in another corner,

you stand with your girlfriend.
You see me watch you.
You smile, raise your left hand

in a tiny wave, meek
and mild. And I'm thinking
of you as the priest

you used to be.
Of the crucifix
above the altar where

others kneeled before you,
took the body to bear
within their hungry, open mouths.

Of the Christ on the cross
behind you, his body
of strained muscle taut

against plank and nail,
that heaves an endless,
straining breath.

I'm thinking of what any of us
can tolerate. Of my own body,
of you, of how I am always

falling, then falling again.

Worship Songs for Ambiguous Recipients

I keep trying to find a light,
Melanie and Alison sing,
on my own, apart from you.
We play a tepid cover
of DC Talk's "In the Light,"
and as my fingers slip
from E to F-sharp Jeff steps
toward me behind the Casio—
his bass nearly as tall
as he is—and cocks his eye,
signal for a quick exit
through the kitchen's rear door
after the last chorus,
when Pastor Kurt dims the lights.
What's going on inside of me?
I despise my own behavior.
We're bad examples, cruising together
through the Atlanta suburbs
to McDonalds while the rest
of the youth group shares the Word
and eats Papa Johns pizza baptized

in garlic butter. But they don't
understand the sacrifice I make,
giving myself over to this boy
who does not believe—this boy
God can save in the dark
of my car, the sheen of french fry
grease, the glow of a giant letter
M rounded, pointing to heaven.

Gnostic Gospel

I was watching *Jesus Christ Superstar* (1973, Norman Jewison, dir.), a movie full of beautiful people. Forgive me Lord, for I have sinned.

And I have to tell you, Lord, I wanted the most beautiful person to be you. But it wasn't. You were about to die—you are always about to die.

The Romans beat the bejesus out of you (see *Stations of the Cross: Station #5* on YouTube). As it is written (King James Bible, Oxford edition, book of Luke,

chapter 22, verse 63): And the men that held Jesus mocked him, and smote him. Smote, the past tense of smite. Smite, to hit somebody hard. Or, to affect them

disastrously. Or, to fill somebody with love or longing. I cannot tell you the difference, Lord. The man who beat you was beautiful. Blonde with kind eyes,

warm, the color of tobacco or coffee or earth. I have to say: I understand why you did it, Lord, why you stood there, held your breath, and took your beating.

Prince and the Revelation

Two thousand zero zero, party over, oops, out of time.

- Prince, "1999"

In 1999, Prince repeatedly told the press that he would retire his eponymous hit at the end of the year. "1999" is a 1982 Cold War song about partying (even the gerund sounds dated) through the apocalypse, and on the eve of the new millennium, Prince's decision to never play the song again signaled his perception of its anachronism. His point was not merely that the Cold War was over. At the time, he was also becoming a Jehovah's Witness, and thus backdating the beginning of the End of Days to 1914. On stage, the song went dormant for eight years, reappearing six years into the War on Terror during the tour for the album *Planet Earth.* Glancing toward that war in lyrics that illustrate his larger loss of lyrical prowess—"Imagine sending your first born off to fight a war / With no good reason how it started or what they're fighting for"—the eponymous song on that 2007 album sounded Prince's new eschatological vision: "Planet Earth must now come into the balance with the one." Two visions of the End of Days: one of dancing in the face of destruction, another of reconciling oneself to the singular truth of scripture. He sometimes played both songs in the same set, counterpoising two distinct revelations.

$\sim$

In 2010, my father—white and seven years older than Prince—was diagnosed with throat cancer three days before his brother died of colon cancer, and then diagnosed with an unrelated ocular melanoma a few weeks after the conclusion of chemo and radiation, and then diagnosed with a severe case of diverticulitis that necessitated a bowel resectioning following his recovery from internal ocular radiotherapy. I thought that a God I no longer believed in was trying to kill my father with a horrid combination of grief and fear and pain. But my father thought that the Muslim Brotherhood was infiltrating the White House.

∽

In his book on Prince's cultural iconicity, Touré argues that "1999" sounded the political apathy of a generation growing up under the threat of imminent destruction.[7] Yet Prince has not always take a "partyup" attitude in the face of ruin's forecast. In other songs like "America" and "Sign 'o' the Times," he records a civilization in decline as if he's merely a "reporter" ("Chaos and Disorder"). Occasionally, he's downright conspiratorial, as in these lines from "Dreamer": "While the helicopter circles us, / This theory's getting deep / Think they're spraying chemicals over the city / While we sleep." "Dreamer" and "Planet Earth" come from more recent, much less popular albums, Prince having gradually lost touch, in Touré's analysis, with the national zeitgeist in the late eighties. In 1988, if one can be precise, with the release of the album *Lovesexy*.

Opening with the lyric "I know there is a heaven. / I know there is a hell. / Listen to me people. / I gotta story to tell," *Lovesexy*, Touré writes, "is Prince's most evangelical album during his zenith."[8] It spreads the Gospel according to Prince: a Gospel of salvation and sex—of sex as salvation—forged in a childhood of Seventh-Day Adventism and, if a song like "Sister" is to be believed, incestuous training in the *ars erotica*. On his way to becoming an artist whose "best days" are widely considered to be behind him, Prince has become more evangelical still, albeit less pornographic. The man who in 1992 could still write "Sexy MF" no longer curses. He witnesses door-to-door. Prince has fallen out of time.

∽

My first revelation that I was falling for Prince came a few years before "1999" was set to expire. I stumbled upon his 1995 album *The Gold Experience* and its single "The Most Beautiful

Girl in the World." Those mid-nineties albums—those three attempts to satisfy a soured contract with Warner Brothers (*The Gold Experience*, along with 1994's *Come* and 1996's *Chaos and Disorder*), and one celebration of that contract's end (1996's *Emancipation*)—brought me to the altar of the Artist where I still worship today. Other albums contain better music, but these albums composed the soundtrack of my first love affair. In the mid-nineties, I did not countenance Prince's vision of the divine sanction of extramarital eroticism. Yet I found his music liberating, crushing, all the more so because the boy I had a crush on at the time also developed a crush on Prince.

Entangled in my fandom are memories of us absconding on the church service after we had played our parts in the church band, of driving around Atlanta white-boy raping to *The Gold Experience*'s "P Control," of catching whiffs of his brown, curly hair with its hint of cat litter and smelling the sheets on my bed after he had slept in them. Entangled are memories of how he stood naked outside the bathroom door and what he didn't say when he said that I was the only person he would feel comfortable cuming with. Entangled are feelings of freedom I now know to be an effect of the deployment of sexuality as something revealed or concealed—a deployment from which Prince derived what Foucault calls the "speaker's benefit" of taboo utterance.[9] But this knowledge does not diminish my memory of a feeling of liberty occasioned by transgression. No less a Christian when he passed everything having to do with sex through the endless mill of speech than when he became a Jehovah's Witness and started exercising discretion, Prince can almost bring the feeling back.

～

Prince's songs are replete with references to baptismal waters.[10] *Purple Rain*'s title track is the most obvious example, but see too *Emancipation*'s "The Holy River." I remember awaiting the beginning of the apocalypse as I swam along the bottom of a blue-tiled pool in early September 1988. I wondered if and when, because I had been baptized, God would rapture me.

～

The artist who imagines being someone's girlfriend remains a conduit to a past that I try to mine for the materials of queer invention. Yet Prince's high-heeled walk down the fine line between desiring and being a woman is not what I now find most queerly appealing. For me, his primary queer appeal is the self-historical one of returning me to a past where I walk in school-uniform brown loafers down, and sometimes cross, the thin line between friendship and eroticism; where I feel intensely a desire I do not know how to name; where I do not want to give my desire the name my faith tells me is a sin; where, in a fit of supreme teenage melodrama, I feel this pleasure, this desire, this pain so apocalyptically that, one day, I nearly die. Prince conjures the experience of desire as queer—a desire related to but, in its definitional and temporal aporia, distinct from my mere faggotry.

He plays in my head when, lonely in a long-distance relationship, I ask friends to spend the night, and they agree. After a bath, we're just going to fall asleep.

Portrait of Will as Billy Joel

In the basement of the split-level ranch
he shares with Howard, Will plays Billy Joel
on the upright piano. I sit beside him on the bench.
Chide, *There's an old man sitting next to me.*
We laugh because it's four-thirty on a Tuesday.
Sing me a song, I tell him. And Will doesn't,
but instead tells me about the boy in high school
he played piano for, interrupted with lines
one of us can remember. *He always smelled
like cat litter.* A sigh. *La la la, di di da, da.*
I try to imagine Will so smitten, which isn't hard.
We're both men at a piano bench stricken
with a hearty adoration, with a dear love of comrades.
Milton, the basset hound, saunters over and sits
at our bare feet. We're all sharing a drink
we do not know what to call. Will strikes a chord
loudly, "Captain Jack," and turns to me, *Jesus,
Tuesday night and you're still hangin' around?*

How to Make a Mixed Tape

1—Meet a boy
        online and think
of him as a fish
          to be netted,
      his shiny scales
      of armor
          only penetrable
by your taste in retrograde
      pop music
      from the mid-
      to late-'90s.

2—Take the boy
      to coffee
      to dinner
      to cinema
      to drinks
      to walk
      to museum
      to bed
      to shower
      because
      a fish must never veer too far
      from water and a boy
      is better to bed again
      when clean.
      Take the boy.

3— On your second date
        explain you're making him
        a mixed tape. By this point
                you should know
        at least four songs
you want to be on this mix,
        and now gauging
        his reaction to this, compile
        your list as if the sun
        will not rise again without
                your music
        serving as its narrative arc.

3.5, or, a few notes on that which must be excluded—Any song
about a breakup, a death, a parent, a child, Jesus, or a butterfly.
This eliminates the entire catalogs of Alanis Morissette, Jason
Mraz, Mariah Carey. You are allowed two songs of irony, and
thus must choose wisely. No Goo Goo Dolls and no Taylor
Swift. You are allowed one cover of "Take My Breath Away,"
and it cannot be the one by Nirvana. No Nirvana. No one
can tell you what to put on the mix. I can tell you what not,
for this mix making, this practice of queer negativity. Is the
practice of making a mixed tape one of negativity, though? Of
what Edelman paints as a "negativity opposed to every form
of social viability?"[11] Is making a mixed tape what mean girl
Regina George calls "social suicide?" Maybe.

4—Proceed
        with caution.
            Choose
        some Sufjan Stevens

        to show you are sincere,
        some Britney Spears
        to show you have a sense
               of humor,
        some Prince, pre-conversion,
        to show you like to jive,
        followed immediately
        by "Sound of Silence."
            This is penance
            for claiming to jive.

5—Show up
        to your third date
with the mixed tape
            in a jewel
case decoupaged
        with funny pictures
that have nothing to do
with you
        or with anything,
like cats and boats
            and birds.
Scratch that. No fucking
birds. This is not a game.

6—Do not text him
            after your date
                        but wait
until the next morning—
last night was wonderful!
enjoying the music? :)
            He will not text you
back.

7—Later that afternoon, panic.
            Text him again.
            And again.
            And finally ask—
            what the fuck dude?
            He will answer—
            sorry, I've been @ work
            all day.

8—Know this: you will feel manic,
            and too embarrassed
to ask him out again.
                        He, of course,
will not be asking you,
                        but will text you
months later, when on the floor
of his car he finds
                        the mixed tape—
            Hey man.
            How are you?
            I'm listening
            to your tape,
            which is great,
            and just wanted
            to say hello.

55

For Boys

I've learned—to fish, to compromise, to hike, to not eat meat, to not eat dairy, to not eat, to purge, to plan, to sustain.

Also—to cook, to clean, to bend over, to bend over backwards, to bend over the back of the sofa, to clean the sofa, to get crabs out of the fabric, to get crabs out of our pubic hair with a fine-tooth comb and permethrin lotion, to permeate hearts, to pretend, to purge again.

Once upon a time I cooked a piece of my pulmonary artery, that which leads to the failing human heart, on the George Forman Grill atop the dung-colored Formica counter. Soon did I learn—artery is not kosher, and the boy was in the method of keeping.

For my father I joined the Boy Scouts of America.

For Cameron I wrote resumés.

For Jared I learned Spanish.

For Zach I feigned interest in Buffy, for my brothers, NASCAR.

For Paul I became brave.

For Jason I assembled a bed from IKEA.

For Robby I accepted Jesus Christ.

For Tyler I pirate the entire catalog of Courtney Love.

For Will, I read Milton and for myself—or my therapist, rather—I make lists, only partial here, because my "mind is its own place, and in itself / Can make a heav'n of hell, a hell of heav'n." Forever and ever, Amen.

Outside a man teaches his son to ride a bicycle. It is yellow with a Spiderman action figure in the spokes of the back tire. There are no training wheels. A-ha! I want to tell the boy, keep on trying. Someday you will look back on all the things you have learned, and why.

Detachment as Buddhist Philosophy

Because I'm not looking for a date,
I give the waiter my number,
tell him I'm here for the weekend
and we should hang out.
It's his hair I like,
wild brown curls
bangs,
dislocation—
I'm from Florida—
and how on Facebook
he holds a balloon
in front of Starbucks.

We meet at Starbucks,
because I'm not looking
for a date
—I'm basically married—
and what I didn't know
until now: he's a Buddhist.
He took a vow
against sexual immorality,
and believes
the mind exists on its own plane
distinct from the body,
which I say is horseshit
because he wants me
to be honest.

Outside Starbucks
on this Atlanta July afternoon
we sweat into our coffee,
take refuge in the mediation center
where he shows me poses.
After Indian food Starbucks again
where he confesses
on the purple couch
problems with detachment,
shows me how to work fingers
into muscles, and places his foot
on my erection.

In my car he leaves
his unseasonal snow hat
so that the next morning
he can text—
Are you smelling my hat?
The one packed
With coffee smell and sweat.
And I don't text back,
because I am.

At the Saturday Farmer's Market

A psychic named Dorothy
asks for five dollars, takes
my left hand into the sweat

of her right one, traces a line,
the one road of love, she tells me,
and yours is very strange indeed,

like there is a lion trapped inside
of you, clawing out through the palm.
Dwell upon this. The lion is sometimes

an unfaced lie—maybe I was twenty
once and in the slow, steady decline
of what seemed a marriage

between two boys who met
in therapy for teenagers
affected by suicide, my brother

and his father. And maybe
he always held this over
me when we fought, always said,

Losing a fucking sibling
cannot even compare to losing
a parent. I believe him, still,

but when he wanted to make
our twosome a triad it was April,
cruelest month. When the dogwoods

bloom in Missouri, their petals
crush under my Converse sneakers
as I walked to campus

to meet a professor, a writer,
a doctor of upstanding citizenry
who maybe asked me into his office,

whom I kissed, maybe, and kicked
the door closed with my foot.
What he did was knock

a picture of his wife and son
from atop the still-frozen lake
of metal desktop. Maybe it broke,

a horrible metaphor, an omen
too clear neither of us chose to see.
When he tied me to his desk chair

using a cornsilk blue necktie
and blindfolded me with a dirty
gym sock, the doctor nibbled down

the entire left side of my boy
body, blew into my ear canal,
traced my trachea with the tip

of his tongue, salted each nipple
and flowed down the river
of happy trail and thigh,

to the edges of my boy toes,
though I couldn't see
any of this, of course,

couldn't see him hold the bottle
of alkyl nitrites to my nose.
Maybe it was then he said, *Boy,*

just breathe. Maybe he swallowed
my cock so whole it hurt,
his teeth rough at the base

and I gasped, gulped
for the air I could not, cannot, get
to fill my empty boy lungs.

So when I tell this story, years
later, maybe I will say it was the other
boy who wrecked our home,

the one for whom I wasn't enough.
Or maybe I will say it was the professor
who asked me into his office,

whom I fucked and was fucked by
for a summer, then the better
part of sophomore year,

whose wife I sat across from
at a Christmas party. *Nice cardigan,*
I told her, knowing the faint stain

on its yellow left sleeve was my cum.
Maybe I will tell it slant, a deflection
from the truth of the matter—

the only common denominator
in all this was me, the boy lion
who roared, yet refuses to show.

Learning to Poem: The Lifespan of a Literary Crush

> A strange den or music room
> childhood
> - Frank O'Hara

Mother works at the Aurora Family Care Center, a low and long brick nursing home on the east side of town, set back from the highway next to a trailer park, shielded from both by two lines of scrubby pine trees. The nursing home is outlined in sidewalks, the sidewalks divided into quadrants by breaks in the concrete. From this I learn about the square, the rectangle, the line, and loveliest: the rhombus. Every morning, Alzheimer's Room 19 marks sections of the sidewalk in chalk and every afternoon I count these. The ones that are marked and the ones that are not. She asks me about simple counting, to produce answers by way of addition and subtraction. She used to be a high school algebra teacher and it is 1989 and George H.W. Bush is president and the San Francisco 49ers just won the Superbowl and Madonna sings "Like a Prayer" which thank god is not "Like a Virgin," and I am five years old, the unexpected son of a nursing director and a government health inspector, counting sections of sidewalk edged in brown and browning crabgrass, wearing acid wash jeans cinched at the ankles and waist.

When your mother is the head nurse, you have certain privileges. I roam freely, areas reserved for staff—kitchen, nurses' station, linen closet—and for residents—dining hall, game room, courtyard. The land here is parched, Father says, and the pine trees, the grasses, the shrubs and the ivy in the courtyard show the effects of a spring that never came. A warm winter that, without warning, is now an endless summer. When Orderly, the only black person in my world, takes her smoke breaks in the courtyard, I watch her five-minute liturgies from behind a cluster of bushes nearby, the bushes where I bury quarters Diabetic Room 45 gives me to fetch her peppermints from my mother's purse. By July, I will be able to buy the Pink Jubilee 25th Anniversary Barbie at Wal-Mart, the one Father refuses to buy me.

The world outside this building displays every sign of natural, brown death; the inside is all artificial, white life. White walls! White tiles! White florescent! Mother's white shoes and white uniform and how everything on laundry day smells of Clorox! I love the Clorox smell. When I take home the Bush-Hidden Quarters, I lock myself in the bathroom, pull the stepstool to the sink and fill it with hot water and bleach, just as I have seen Mother do. I remove the Bush-Hidden Quarters from my backpack, the Kansas City Chiefs backpack I did not want, and wash them. My thumbs rub again and again across the face of George Washington. My skin puckers where it rubs the quarters, under the conditions of bleach and steaming water. In my room the Bleach-Clean Quarters gleam in the Kraft Mayonnaise jar where I keep them. The jar I keep hidden in my closet, buried amongst Legos, a baseball bat, and the My Buddy Doll that now wears the sweatshirt I have outgrown, a red hoodie that says *Daddy's #1 All Star*. I will never remember wearing this sweatshirt, though pictures are able to dispel myth into fact. At night, I lie on the floor of my closet and smell the Bleach-Clean Quarters as they pass through my fingers back into their jar, as the sheen of them catches light from the flashlight I have stolen from my brother and brought into the closet. Light catches and refracts in the dark of the closet.

When your mother is the head nurse, you have certain privileges. I am five years old and in those hours where my parents' jobs overlap, I have innumerable surrogates—Line Cook, who makes his tattoo mermaid dance for me in the kitchen just off the dining hall; Alzheimer's Room 19; Diabetic Room 45; the *Designing Women*—Dixie Carter, Delta Burke,

Annie Potts, and Jean Smart—in the TV room; the bushes where I keep Bush-Hidden Quarters; sometimes my sister, when she does not have cheerleading or college prep or boyfriends. But my favorite surrogate is Mr. Williams.

For most of his life, Mr. Williams has been a drama teacher in New York City. Back at our house, I pull the atlas, the one from State Farm Insurance, from Father's bookshelf. This book I am allowed. Unlike the Bible, the one my mother reads to me before bed, where people die and then ride back on a cloud of black fire atop a black horse and then the black book is shut, edged again in gold and put high on a shelf named No: Do Not Touch, or Never. I open to the State of New York and there above the smallness of Syracuse is a detail of *The City*. I trace the island of it.

More than miles separate *The City* from Aurora, Missouri.

Mr. Williams is here to die. This is a nursing home— everyone is here to die, and sometimes, as is the case with Mr. Williams, the dying does not come steady. Not like a train. More like a raft on a great river of white water, where the floating is lackadaisical for mile after mile and then drops, sometimes without warning, foot after freefalling foot. This is AIDS, which a five year old has no concept of; this is 1989 when few do. Mr. Williams was born near here in his parents' bed, in a home that has long since been razed. Mr. Williams has come back to these Ozark Mountains, to the place of his birth, to die.

It is Tuesday, an afternoon in May just before summer. Like most other Tuesdays, I have watched *Designing Women* with Mr. Williams. I walk beside his wheelchair and like this, we travel back to his room—place of innumerable wonders among the doldrums of a Midwestern nursing home. At the end of the hall is the private suite where Mr. Williams spends his days dying, though I have little concept of this. No way of comprehension. Perhaps this is why he enjoys my company, why he invites me into the bedroom he has filled with prints emblazoned MoMA and Whitney and Guggenheim. With a throw blanket made of African tribal fabric. With a record player and neat, alphabetized rows of vinyl. Our favorite, Ella Fitzgerald. And books. I am most amazed by the books. Are these forbidden? I know few beyond the atlas and the Bible.

Yet, I know much of possibility and impossibility. I am five years old.

Mr. Williams is going blind. I read aloud to him every afternoon, practice for school sanctioned by both Mother and Mr. Williams. When I stumble on a word I do not know, which is often, Mr. Williams bids me spell the word aloud to him. He teaches me to pronounce it and gives a definition I do not or cannot understand. It is an afternoon just before summer, extra ordinary, the interim that only a balmy Tuesday in May is able to be, in a place by a trailer park and a highway, surrounded by scrubby pines and outlined in gray concrete that seems endless. I pull a book off the shelf, little with an electric orange cover.

Lunch Poems, by Frank O'Hara.

I am five years old and it is the first book of poetry I encounter. The words in their queer combinations hold innumerable possibility, though I understand neither these combinations nor these possibilities yet. I am five years old and something sparks. Mr. Williams listens as I read aloud to him what Frank O'Hara has written: "Mothers of America / let your kids go to the movies!" I am, unbeknownst, in love. I am, unbeknownst, learning from my forefathers an aesthetic of queerness, a lineage, a heritage, a bloodline. Much later, in the first year of my PhD, I will read José Esteban Muñoz on O'Hara, on the quotidian nature of a poem like "Having a Coke with You," which signifies, Muñoz explains, "a vast lifeworld of queer relationality, an encrypted sociality, and a utopian potentiality."[12] The queer utopia is always on the horizon, Muñoz will use O'Hara to explain. That which has always been here, like O'Hara in my own life, strangely; that which has already passed, like O'Hara, tragically, on a Fire Island beach, struck by a dune buggy in the hazy morning hours of July 24, 1966; and that which has yet to come, generations of poets who will read O'Hara, who might read me and all the queer brothers and sisters who write now and have yet to write.

I am twenty-eight years old now and pull a book off the shelf, little, with an electric orange cover. When I walk to catch a bus or to buy a newspaper, I count the squares of sidewalk, adding and subtracting them in my head. I am twenty-eight years old and I live in Washington, DC. Comfortably, though it is not home. I write poems. Now I am queer and can tell you about AIDS. I can give you the definitions to words, which I do not know where—but I do know—I have learned. I am twenty-eight now and I listen to Ella Fitzgerald. Clorox is one of my favorite smells. I am twenty-eight and I go to the movies with friends or with boyfriends. Or sometimes I go alone. It is nice to be alone but not alone in the dark. I think of Mr. Williams. I think of Mother, thankful she let me go to the movies. I think of Frank.

I am twenty-eight years old and I pull a book off the shelf. *Lunch Poems*, by Frank O'Hara.

After Watching 10 Things I Hate About You, *Echo Writes Narcissus a Poem in the Vein of Julia Stiles*

I hate the way you talk to me,
and the way you tell me I'm poor.

I hate the way you roll your eyes,
but not that you're a voyeur.

I hate that you'd like to walk me
through a field of wildflowers
                 and then check my legs,
       my ears, my ass, for ticks.

I hate that because you can't touch
my body, I know this: you check
              my poems
              for ticks.

I hate the way you LOLz at me,
how you always say, *Don't know, don't care.*

I hate that you tell me to read *Othello*
when I want to read *Midsummer Night's*.

       That I want to rename you
       Demetrius. That I want to say,

       I am your spaniel, and, Demetrius,
       the more you beat me I will fawn on you.

I hate that I fawn on you.
That I fawn.

Okay, let's tell it slant—grant me this,
        I don't hate you, but I know
        you like to play the hater.

I hate that I only make passes
at boys who wear glasses.

        I hate that you don't like to wear
        your glasses.

        In the bathhouse, I hate
        how my glasses fog with steam.
        I hate mine eyes, which have seen
                        the coming
        of The Lord.

Confession: I hate your obsession
with Brad Paisley
        and I hope it's ironic.
                        Okay, confession:
I don't hate that.
        Or you.
        Not even a little bit.
                        Not even at all.

III: In the Garden, or Before the Fall

> The edgèd steel, by careless chance,
> Did into his own ankle glance,
> And there among the grass fell down
> By his own scythe the mower mown.
>
> - Andrew Marvell, "Damon the Mower"

> I see world-making here as functioning and coming into play
> through the performance of queer utopian memory, that is, a utopia
> that understands its time as reaching beyond some nostalgic past
> that perhaps never was or some future whose arrival is
> continuously belated—a utopia in the present.
>
> - José Esteban Muñoz

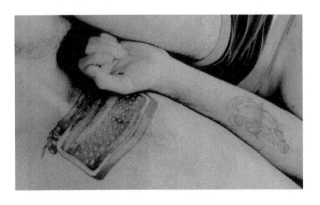

In the Locker Room, My Father

is a god. I wait on the bench below him
like Ares, wrapped in a white towel,
rough cotton, stamped *Smithfield YMCA*.

Steam settles around our collection of feet.
Like this we prepare for war. He tells me:
Son, you will walk away from your home,

from the hearts of your mother and father.
I will command this. You will walk in search
of the Mississippi and along the way, become

an avid St. Louis Cardinals fan. You will
learn how to fill a pipe with fine tobacco.
How to give a woman your phone number

with grace. When you reach the muddy banks,
you will swim to an island and come back
where nothing is the same. Water drips

onto the breadth of my father's thighs,
onto the lack of my own. How old am I?
Nine? Ten? My father sighs and tells me:

Or son, you will take to men. They will take
to you and you will become their prophet,
but also their sacrifice, their burnt offering.

On the Anniversary of My Infidelity

One year, five months, eighteen
days after my infidelity we text back
and forth about insurance as I ride

the elevator to my sixth-floor office.
The elevator stops at five,
goes down again as I lose signal,

your assurance, and question
your strategy to save us
five hundred dollars annually.

At two the door opens to
a bike, this self-assured boy with red
bed head and hirsute hands tattooed.

I slam emergency stop,
with nothing assured slam
myself into him, our limbs falling

into bike frame, us to the floor,
to the basement of the building
unsure if we'll ever rise again.

Up again only when I've tasted
inside his cheeks, greased
my thigh with chain oil.

I make room for this boy,
ride to five and take the stairs.
Reassured and walk down.

On Faggot: A Travelogue

At the cottage of Anne Hathaway, which is in the town of Stratford-upon-Avon, which is in Warwickshire County, which is in the West Midlands, which is in England, which is in the United Kingdom, a portly tour guide points to a fireplace in the kitchen: *this is where they burned the faggots.*

She continues with the tour. *Here is the bed, his second best, which William Shakespeare gave his dear wife Anne. Notice how it is short. In those times, they slept not flat on their backs, but somewhere between upright and reclining. This was out of an old fear: if Lucifer saw one lying flat, he would think one was dead and sweep in during the night to capture their soul.* I notice the intricate embroidery, yellow and mint green, on a tapestry down the hall and think to myself, "Jesus, Duane, you're such a faggot."

The *Oxford English Dictionary* lists 26 words with fag- as their root, from the late eighteenth century colloquial verb *fag*—that which causes weariness; hard work, toil, drudgery, fatigue—to the 1724 Germanic use of *fagotto*, a musical term that implies with bassoon.

At the Pittsburgh International Airport, our flight to London via Newark is cancelled. We are shuttled to a nearby Comfort Inn and eat dinner at a dive bar next door. The place smells familiar and a friend turns to me: *it smells like a backwater queer bar in here!* Yes! Exactly. Like the first gay bar I went to: Martha's Vineyard on Olive Street in Springfield, Missouri. When I was a heterosexual, I went there one night with co-workers, drank too much, blacked out atop a table, and woke up a homosexual. The next night, I returned newly queer, and met a prince—this is when I believed in fairy tales. What is that smell? Cigarettes, spilled vodka, and lube? Maybe. But this isn't a gay bar.

I walk to the bathroom where beside the urinal, someone has drawn a cock on the wall. Above this, someone has sprawled the word faggott with two t's, which I take to mean an overzealous faggot.

~

In his *Annotations*, John Keene says "Missouri, being an amalgam of nearly every American region, presents the poet with a particularly useful analogue." I try to understand this, but cannot. From London, I email to ask my mother, deep in the Missouri of both geography and metaphor. She, too, is baffled. One afternoon, as I stroll the cobble-stoned alleys of Soho, the sentiment is all I can think of, though its meaning is still unclear.

~

Three movies terrified me as a child. First, *Return to Oz*. This was 1989 and I was five years old. My sister, age seventeen, brought the VHS home from Aurora Video Source, where she worked on the weekends. In the movie Dorothy, somehow both younger and British, which is why I remember this now, visits an insane asylum. For a year, I could not sleep alone. When I am eight, Uncle Dennis is brought to us, dying from AIDS. The same sister, twenty now, tries to explain and shows me *And the Band Played On*. Among other things, I think the movie is unfair to the Reagan administration and that two men kissing results in death. Which is why, as I watch *Legends of the Fall* in the basement during high school, I am scared for my life when Brad Pitt, shirtless, wades into a rushing creek. I kiss my girlfriend, but think of him.

~

My favorite fag- root in the dictionary is *faggoteer*, one who makes faggots. British faggoteers—David Bowie, David Beckham, The Spice Girls, Charles Darwin, Julie Andrews, Angela Lansbury, imperialism, Winnie the Pooh, rugby, and parliamentary procedure. Also—Oscar Wilde, Elton John, George Michael, and Harry Potter, though it is unclear whether or not one can be both a fag and make further faggotry. And yes, Diana, Princess of Wales.

Also worth consideration, American faggoteers— Madonna; Walt Whitman; Calvin Klein; Michael Jordan; Bob Dylan, and more so, his son Jakob; Starbucks; Levi Strauss; Kurt Cobain; and Brad Pitt. Also, Patsy Cline, the cast of *Friends*, and Hillary Clinton.

∿

In London, Prince William prepares to marry Kate Middleton. On the television in our hotel room, Andy and I watch oodles of gay men discuss every minutiae of the wedding. In this way, gay men are commodities. *Yes, Alexander McQueen's protégé could be designing Kate's dress. No, the Queen will not upstage the bride. Prince Harry should keep his speech short. Hats are appropriate. White lilies and tulips would be nice. Stringed quartet, not jazz band. Undoubtedly, Princess Diana would not approve.* Oscar Wilde, from the grave, "the highest as the lowest form of criticism is a mode of autobiography."[13] That sounds about right. Wayne says all this "proves that fashion ideas come from fags watching revivals and paying acute attention to fugue and fatigue"; his alliteration is quite lovely.[14] I am a confused commodity, though I begin to understand British queens. And American queens. And that everyone must weigh in.

∿

My least favorite fag-rooted word is *fage*, a verb, the action of coaxing or deceiving; a fiction or deceit.

The Globe Theater is a complete fage. A modern recreation that opened in 1997, the new Globe is believed to be "very similar" to that of Shakespeare's construction, though it is located 754 feet from the original. Our tour guide is an allegory, a tall drink of water on these banks of the Thames. He is married, presumably heterosexual, and at every joke he cracks, I laugh a little too loudly. In this way, I am a cliché, another gay man drawn to an unattainable straight man. It is all language, all syntax. In a hall with posters for Shakespeare's plays, I ask the guide his favorite. He points to *As You Like It*, and says *all the world's a stage, and I, just one of its players.*

∿

77

At the Bodleian Library, I pick up a reprint of a 1942 pamphlet from the United States War Department: *Instructions for American Servicemen in Britain.* Uncle Sam explains "YOU are going to Great Britain as part of an Allied offensive—to meet Hitler and beat him on his own ground. For the time being you will be Britain's guest."[15] What follows is sage advice.

I imagine my Uncle William, not a fag like Shakespeare, fresh out of training. He was likely given this pamphlet. Probably carried it alongside letters from his young wife, my Aunt Marilyn. On page five, as he sailed from the deep of Missouri to New York and on still to London, he likely read "The British have phrases and colloquialisms of their own that may sound funny to you. You can make just as many boners in their eyes."[16] Did he laugh, as I do now? Or did he, a soldier in the war machine that became the Greatest Generation, take his boners more seriously?

$\sim$

In May of 1780, Madame D'Arblay, English playwright and laborious conversationalist, wrote in her diary, "I felt horribly fagged," which means wearied out, excessively fatigued. In February of 1992, Marvin Willhite, Jr., methamphetamine dealer and my brother, also became *fagged.*

I will say this exactly one time. My father, our brother Randy, Marvin, and I had lunch at Boxcar Bar-b-que. This is at 1131 North Grant Avenue in Springfield, Missouri. I do not like bar-b-que, and told them as much, pouting through the entire meal. As we leave, Marvin grabs my arm, *don't be such a little faggot.*

I don't say that because it is sad. I say it because it's confusing to me now. Which faggot did he mean? The 1700 use, meaning a person temporarily hired to supply a deficiency at the muster? To bind hand and foot? Any number of bundles—steel rods, wooden sticks, planks? The practice of burning heretics?

I lied. I will say it again. My brother called me faggot in the parking lot and two days later, killed himself—this was with a shotgun in his mouth in the back bedroom of his trailer.

$\sim$

When we visit the ancient Roman bathhouse, I am not interested in the coins, or the curve of stone archways described as *revolutionary*. But I do want to understand. What did they wear here? Were the sex acts performed in the open, or in dark corners? How did bathhouses evolve? My questions go unanswered. In the hot pool below the ten o'clock sun, I dip my hand into the water. A tour guide yells from across the hall, *stop!* Too much is forbidden, and the rules go unexplained.

Later, in London, I go below the street to use the public restroom. There are five urinals, four of which are full. I pull into the empty parking space. Next to me four men masturbate, tugging their erect, uncircumcised cocks towards the metal pool of toilet. This is like when Wayne says, "I am confused about what's contemporary and what's outdated. I am confused about the spirit of the age."[17] The men glare at me, annoyed that I do not join in? And this is progress—less is forbidden, but the rules still go unexplained.

∽

I should be interested in countryside. At the home of William Wordsworth, I should walk through the gardens and consider the foliage, the abundant daffodils and sizeable wisteria bushes that grow along nineteenth-century stone fences. But for the last few days, since we've arrived in England, all I can think about is urinals. I take pictures of them at London Heathrow, Shakespeare's birthplace, the Jane Austen Center, sundry pubs and town squares, McDonald's, and now, the visitor center of William Wordsworth's expansive estate, home of *the* quintessential Romantic poet. Am I romanticizing piss? The places we piss? Is this a fetish? Is this how obsession feels?

∽

I have a professor who teaches me to write poems. One day I give him one. He says, *I like this, but make it a little more faggy.* I try, but do not know what this means. Later, I add a urinal in the third line of the second stanza to no avail.

∽

The underground bathroom we talked about earlier is not a bathhouse; the comparison was not apt, and I need to rectify this.

So in London, I want to visit a bathhouse. I go to Starbucks and research establishments on my iPhone. I decide on the SaunaBar, near the Covent Garden Tube station at 29 Endell Street. Like the underground bathroom, SaunaBar is subterranean, down a flight of stairs below a yogurt shop. I set rules for myself. Do not judge. Do not have sex. Blend in. Face this fear of knowledge.

The fear comes from the aforementioned movie: *And the Band Played On*, where bathhouses are painted as a breeding ground for AIDS. I still become nervous in the locker room. But then I remember Anjelica Huston was in that film, though this was before I knew her as a goddess.

The clerk at SaunaBar takes my wallet and cell phone. He hands me a towel and locker key, saying, *have fun, lil' guy*. The rest is mostly uninteresting. There is one attractive man—mid 30s, blonde, slim but muscled physique. Let's call him Evan. Evan probably swims a lot. Evan probably has a corporate job in the nearby financial district. How else can this be said? From four feet away, I watch Evan fuck a man. Evan smiles at me, looks for me to cheer him on. I watch. Evan finishes and I follow him to the changing area, where we both dress. From a distance, I follow Evan above ground, onto the street, around the corner, into the arms of his wife and child. I do not know how else to say this.

I duck into a nearby record store and thumb a rare Cyndi Lauper vinyl. Alongside Anjelica Huston, I believe she is a goddess.

∿

Whereas I call them goddess, my therapist calls the women in my life like Cyndi Lauper and Anjelica Huston escape artists. This man used to be my therapist. I call him a prick.

∿

This etymology is a maze. Consider the 1853 *faggery*, or system of *fagging* at public schools. Then *fagging*, the action of the verb *fag*, which probably means "to beat." Another interesting definition, however, is "to cut corn with a sickle and a hooked stick." Jimmy fagged corn, and I don't care because Jimmy is an Aquarius and too blond for my tastes.

In a tongue-in-cheek sex book I picked up in the bathroom at the Queenschilling in Bristol, we are told "fags often suffer from obsessions with men they have never met." Yes; that's the Jimmy we just talked about. Who is he? Maybe Jimmy Carter or James Dean. Not James Franco, who is not too anything except too perfect.

Somewhere on the internet someone says that *faggot*, when translated from French to English, can mean *meatball*. I cannot establish this as fact, but in 1862, Mrs. H. Wood exclaims in a letter to her friend Mrs. Hallib, "Mine is a fagging profession!" Her profession, sadly, is unknown. This was in Victorian England. Was she the butcher, the baker, or the candlestick maker? Or was she of noble birth: a duchess, a countess, or a baroness? So much is lost in bad record keeping.

~

I think of fagging professions today: barista, psychoanalyst, and gym teacher. Maybe this is wishful thinking. In the west of England, we spend a day in Bath. I visit Colonna & Smalls Espresso Room at 12a Princes Street, a small alleyway behind the Royal National Hospital For Rheumatic Diseases. For an hour and a half, I speak with Maxwell, the fourth best barista in the United Kingdom according to the World Barista Championship, a subsidiary of the Specialty Coffee Associations of Europe and America. In an hour, I've thought of all the ways I could move here, date Maxwell and live happily. Which is to say, hold Maxwell's hand and write him poems. In the next half hour, I've thought of how ridiculous this is. That Maxwell is not even gay. That this obsession has gone far enough.

It is difficult being human sometimes; this living is *fagging*, in this sense, the action of wearing oneself. Making oneself the *fag-end*, the last part or remnant of anything, after the best has been used.

Sex & The Linguistic Act

In the mountains of North Carolina
a boy wades into a creek
wearing nothing but a faded
Dylan t-shirt. His father's, he tells me,
and I believe him because
I have the faith of a mustard seed
that with enough faith this boy
and I are going to have sex.
When he reaches his arms high
as if in praise, I kneel as if in prayer,
taking him into my mouth
so he's rooted there
like a water cress roots
into the creekbed. When I look up,
he is smiling down at me,
as if he is his namesake, Adam,
the first man, smiling down at Eve,
as if I am her, the handmaiden,
the help mate, I've always been taught
as a boy. As if we are still boys, this man
and I, he raises his foot and splashes
me playfully. I stifle a laugh with his cock
in my mouth and look up. The afternoon
sun filters through the canopy of oak
trees rooted here at the base

of a mountain to which I will never care
enough to know the name. Later, when
I have dropped the boy off at his college
apartment, I text Will—*you know,*
there are a few things I am bad at—
who replies—*like making life choices?*
Sometimes, yes, like loving a boy
on a fleeting afternoon in a rushing creek.
Loving him and misnaming this,
just like Adam, charged with naming
all things, surely making a few mistakes—
Oak tree. Sunlight. Love. Boy. Afternoon.

On a Monday, We Talk About Our Testicles As The Mirror Stage

Despite how many times I turn
its terracotta pot, the jade plant

above my desk will always reach
for the sun beyond the open window.

But I'm tired. I'm tired of making
metaphor, of making meaning.

Jiminy cricket. Being a poet
is hard motherfucking work

sometimes. Sometimes it's too
easy though—we're talking

about our balls—I can't make
this shit up—when descended

your left testicle is much longer
than your right. When descended

my right testicle is much longer
than my left. Your predicament

results from an enlarged vas
deferens, the tube that carries

sperm from your cajones through
your Johnson into the world.

Mine, from a simple baseball
injury at age 12, when I squatted

behind homeplate and caught
pitch after pitch from Marc Kaufman.

Why are we talking about our balls?
Is this the prophecy Foucault

gave us—*You will seek to transform
your desire, your every desire,*

into discourse. We're tired.
We're tired and when our iPhones

blaze with another text message,
about balls or boys or desires

it's like a poem that writes itself,
but when I look up, the jade plant

needs turned again. I turn it, do what
neither of us is able to stop doing.

Later that Monday, The Ego Arises

No need to make metaphor
when everything already is.
At 14, I thought I had testicular cancer.
The doctor twirled my right ball
in his left hand and shook his head.
No, he told me, *no need to worry.*
Years later, another doctor—a beautiful one
specializing in gay men's health—marveled
at my testicle as textbook. He wished
his students were there to see. I stared down
at his head in my crotch and felt sick
to my stomach. That mirror is a metaphor,
I think. That consolidation of a self-image
with parts one would cut off, parts measured
against the images in anatomy books
and porn. Not that I could stomach
the cutting, a surgery that could fix this.
None of us can. Before long into evening,
before beds cradle us, ground us
in Washington and South Carolina,
iPhones blaze, another text. You suggest
photographs. I think of one: our balls crushed
together, mass of hairy chicken skin.
To the left, curious, ugly lumps. To the right,
a long excess of skin, as if you were never cut.

On the Origin of A Sexual Aim

> I shall at this point introduce two technical terms.
> Let us call the person from whom sexual attraction
> proceeds the *sexual object* and the act toward
> which the instinct tends the *sexual aim*.
>
> - Freud, *Three Essays on the Theory of Sexuality*

When I first realized that the exigencies of the body could both frustrate and feed the exigencies of desire, I was taking, despite what had been my best and most painful efforts at clenching, an exceptionally loud shit in the bathroom off the living room where sat the boy, four years my junior, whom I had been trying for the better part of two years to seduce, although I never quite knew that seduction was my goal, or he its object. The house smelled like cat litter, always and throughout, even though the litter box was confined to the laundry room. The smell stuck in his hair. My concern, however, was not just that I was adding to the smells of the house, but, more unforgivably, that I was interrupting the sounds—the sound of the television show playing in the living room where he sat with his mother, and the sound of the dryer tumbling laundry that would also smell like cat litter. I was ruining any chance I had of maintaining my friendship by noisily voiding my bowels—the somatic storehouse of my desire for him.

I was wrong, of course, but not about somatic storehouses of desire. Freud's silly theory was, for me, entirely apropos of my experiences in that bathroom with its cold and clinical, white-grouted, white tile: "The contents of the bowels, which act as a stimulating mass upon a sensitive portion of mucous membrane, behave like forerunners of another organ, which is destined to come into action after a phase of childhood."[18]

87

Simply detach childhood from age, or allow it to recur, to fold back on itself.

Loud shitting didn't end our friendship. The trauma of sitting on that toilet, of finally emerging from the bathroom and saying that I had to go home, right now, has nonetheless so crushed time for me that I can't remember any longer whether it was before or after that event that we took a shower together. He was straight, definitely. He had a girlfriend, whom he assured me had just that afternoon given him a blowjob. But whether it was his idea or mine, or something that emerged out of the shared mind I took as a sign of how "deep" and "intense" our friendship was, we took advantage of his mother's absence and decided to watch porn. He was too young to go into the store. Thus I went, stomach wrenching, and he sat in the car, having told me he didn't care what I chose. In deference to his desire, but not really, I chose something with women. And what started in the living room—clothes shedding, penises hardening with a shame that fed arousal—moved soon to the basement, with its long L-shaped couch and larger TV. I came once, quickly, and just as quickly cleaned myself, wrapping myself in a blanket. He didn't cum, just sunk back into the pillows and stroked.

What followed is a lesson in how sexual aims get fixed, stuck in time. When he said he wanted to shower, he also said I should keep him company. In the bathroom, in the steam, we compared, but he shook his head when I asked if I could put my mouth on his cock. Instead, he took my hand and wrapped it around him. He came on the shower curtain, then stepped out. *Sorry to cum and run*, he said almost soundlessly. *It's just not for me.*

How to Do it Yourself

1—Commit yourself
to learning something new—
How to Play the Piano
(for middle- to upper-class white boys).

2—Find a teacher who tasks you,
Michelle Pfeiffer as a dominatrix,
who knows when you don't drill
and makes you drill
until you're back where you started,
fumbling through "Michael, Row Your Boat Ashore."

3—Draw the circle of fifths
with a compass and a protractor.
Tape this to your bathroom mirror,
where you study as you brush your teeth,
the paper wrinkling with shower steam.

4—Become obsessed.
Save up your lawnmowing money.
Buy a keyboard. At night, practice in your room.
Harbor secret fantasies about being Billy Joel.

5—Improvise with the chord progression
to "We Didn't Start the Fire"
but fail to remove the jackhammer melody.
Shift scenes.

Imagine playing "She's Always a Woman"
for your best friend's girl,
which you will when your fingers learn
to move from 4 on C to 5 on E flat.

6—Do not play Billy Joel in public.
Develop instead an impression
to amuse your friends.
Tori Amos straddling the piano bench,
playing minor chord progressions
and moaning the sounds of orgasm.
Do not mock Tori in private.

7—Allow a decade to pass.
Find new obsessions
with brief interludes of reinterest in the piano.
Listen to your taskmaster of a therapist
when she tells you you're being evasive.

8—When a cute boy asks if you play,
put right-hand 1 on G sharp, 2 on B,
3 on D sharp and 5 on F sharp.
Left-hand 1 on E and 5 on E,
when a cute boy asks you if you play.
You will have forgotten what chord you're making
or what key you're in.
A song from the book hidden inside
your piano bench: "I Wanna Be Your Lover."

Roundtable, Part Two

or, The Miltonist Questions Contemporary Literature

The Miltonist throws his hands up in the air and sighs—
Why are all of you
so…
so…
um…
recent?

The contemporary poets, led by E. Bishop with a staff not unlike
the one Moses carried, leave the room in a huff. A. Ginsberg,
however, is left behind, asleep or meditating under the table.

The Miltonist unpacks a stack of books and pours each book a
cup of tea. The books turn into their authors, and it is not unlike
a Ren Fair except there are no chicken legs.

The Miltonist asks—
What say all of you?

G. Chaucer clears his throat—
Now for the love of God and of Seint John,
Leseth no tyme as ferforth as ye may!

W. Wordsworth touches his temple—
A poet!—He hath put his heart to school,
Nor dares to move unpropped upon the staff

O. Wilde interrupts him—
Oh hey gurl! How big
is this staff?

E. Dickinson faints.

J. Keats fans E. Dickinson with an embroidered hanky pulled
from his right sleeve (hunter green, signifying orphan boy
seeking a daddy). He shoots a look at O. Wilde—
the great end
Of poesy, that it should be a friend
To soothe the cares, and lift the thoughts of man.

O. Wilde rolls his eyes—
Bitch,
Please.

The Miltonist becomes visibly worried this is getting out of
control.

W. Shakespeare tilts his head—
O, sure I am the wits of former days

> J. Keats uses the hand not fanning E. Dickinson to rub W.
> Shakespeare's leg.

W. Shakespeare jolts up—
O, my boy, how many times must you hear
that I, unequivocally, am not a flaming queer?

W. Whitman shrugs his shoulders—
I proceed for all who are or have been young men,
To tell the secret of my nights and days,
To celebrate the need of comrades.

J. Keats and O. Wilde in unison—
Go home, Walt!

E. Dickinson sits up on her haunches—
Inebriate of air—am I—
And Debauchee of Dew—

W. Wordsworth looks around for support—
Such a shame, all these drunken Americans.

J. Milton rises from his seat, demanding the attention of all in
the room—
So Man, as is most just,
Shall satisfie for Man, be judg'd and die.

E. Dickinson puts up her right hand—
Who runs the world? Girls.

A. Ginsberg, who apparently was meditating this whole time
and not sleeping—
O victory forget your underwear we're free.

A. Ginsberg walks from the room, knocking over a Grecian urn
standing by the door. It shatters.

The Miltonist, E. Dickinson, and W. Shakespeare begin to weep.

J. Keats gasps.

For God, We Break the Rules of Grammar

Second-graders wipe cafeteria tables,
sing "Joy to the World" with Christmas ten days away.
The Lord has come—I sing—
and Mrs. Franklin stops me—
The Lord is come. He is not no longer here.
He is here now as we hoky sandwich crumbs,
watch the third-graders
outside at a recess that for us has come
when we have finished cleaning.

In a fifth-grade classroom soaked with boy smell,
Mrs. Stith explains the present perfect—
the action is over, but it has a present influence.
In a chest of sweat, my heart leaps,
like the Bible says,
with present understanding
of His omnipresence—
For God, we break the rules of grammar.

Having broken unspoken rules,
I write my seventh-grade Bible teacher
Mr. Leatherman an essay about doubt—
I don't want to play Bible Trivia anymore.
And Mr. Leatherman holds me after school

to tell me doubt is the essence of faith,
to come again to the Lord with my doubt.
But I doubt Mr. Leatherman knows
what I doubt. His presence
as I watch Tyler change for gym.
For the punishment has not come.

For what I don't yet know—
in second, fifth, and seventh grades—
is history: the demon who turns doubt to disbelief.
In the eighteenth century, *to be*
functions as an auxiliary verb.
For Isaac Watts, *is come* is perfect present perfect
and refers not to the past,
but to the second coming,
to the future when the Lord is come again.
I have stopped believing in the resurrection,
in the second coming, in the omnipresence
of a God who watches me watching boys.
I have become unsaved,
an unbeliever who still keeps his room clean
(Proverbs 22:6: *Train up a child
in the way he should go, and when he is old,
he will not depart from it*)
and his heart open
for language—for all I have left of God,
for all I have left to worship.

Hibernation: Three Scenes

I. Winter, 1952

Frank O'Hara walks into the office, complaining.
Save yourself, the Psychiatrist tells the Poet,
You can't do anything about your mother.
In time, Frank replaces her with Grace
Hartigan, firecracker formerly on the periphery
of the New York School painters O'Hara
considered his closest friends. She
becomes the subject of a short poem:
"For Grace, After a Party," where Frank tells
her, *it was love for you that set me / afire,*
/ and isn't it odd? for in rooms full of / strangers
my most tender feelings / writhe and bear
the fruit of screaming. The faggot, dear Frank,
has a crush on a woman, and isn't it odd?

II. Winter, 1986

It is fate: Eve Sedgwick meets Michael Lynch
at the 1986 MLA Convention. She crushes
hard, first on the signature white glasses
on his face, rushing to buy a matching pair,
and then on the man behind the specs—
Michael, the poet succumbing to AIDS. Spring

comes. They fall in love. They lie together
and Eve, returning to Eden, the garden
that is always in the future, pontificates—
When I am in bed with Michael, our white glasses
line up neatly on the night table and I always
fantasy that I may walk away wearing the wrong
ones.[19] Eve is married, yet denies no one, not
Adam, nor Michael, nor the woman bearing white.

III. Winter, 2013

And isn't odd? When I walk into a classroom,
I sit next to a different Michael? That he smiles
at me? That I read O'Hara & Sedgwick as I crush
into him, into this gay boy with an eight-month
girlfriend? That I cannot touch him or be touched,
so I take him in the daylight to a coffeeshop?
That when I sit across from him as he reads,
I pretend to read, too, but instead read the map
that is his eyelashes and cheekbones and lips?
That I cannot tell where the map two boys
are reading will end? That when he removes
his glasses and places them next to my own
on the table between us, that I, for a moment,
hope I will walk away wearing the wrong ones?

Rerun

for Bryan

It's the episode where Samantha pees
on somebody while they're having sex,
you say. And I think I remember,
Oh. He's a midget, right? But he's not
a little person, you tell me,
That's two seasons later.
And we're in two different states,
your Arkansas burning against
my Washington. I was never good
at geography. Or this: at twenty
I told a friend, *If ever I start*
comparing myself to one of the ladies
from Sex and the City, it's time
to start therapy again.
How much difference, though,
eight whole years, an almost
decade, two graduate degrees,
three boyfriends, almost
rehab, one more almost dead
brother, two mother heart attacks,
and a move to a town in the mountains
at the confluence of three great rivers
can make. How much changes,

or doesn't, we're telling ourselves
over the electrons of cell phone
towers and radio waves, tributaries
and the flight paths of migratory birds.
Or: the thing that makes geography
irrelevant now, makes it possible
for your Arkansas to burn
into my Washington. Sometimes,
it is like this: two boys watch reruns
of *Sex and the City,* fourteen years
after the show first appeared.
They compare themselves to the ladies—
I am so Sam in this one, you say.
*Right! And when Big breaks Carrie's
heart that seventh time, I'm definitely her,*
I jump in—but here is the truth,
said plainly. The boys are the boys
they want to be tonight—those girls
in the shoes they could never afford.

Liturgy

Greased flesh sinking
down into a hole forced open by thin fingers;
feet over head, curved spine,
      knees crushing into forehead;
sweat dripping though hair
      into hole where it mixes with lube
      and saliva
      and still isn't slippery enough so
      you pull out and open the bottle
      and pour it into your hand
      and rub it counter-clockwise
      and push yourself back in;
the stick and the sounds—
      the slapping on the back of my thighs
      as they smack into the front of yours;
the smell of ice cream on your breath,
      in my nose as you pin my ankles
      to the sheets that will need changing;
reaching down to feel you slip;
how I'm going to feel when you finish
      and unfold me;
how you bend to kiss me, the strain
      of your stretch felt in your lips;
how at this angle you slam sooner
      into the curve than when I rode you;

how the deeper into me you go the more
        surfaces you encounter;
the sweat on your palms;
the way your hips press into my ass
        and fuse us desiring machines;
organs and the way yours curves;
the look on your face
        as you tell me without words that you're cuming;
how I cum without any touch and little orgasm,
        spilling into the folds of my stomach;
how you've used me worse than any spaniel;
how after a few moments breath you slacken
        and relax your crush on my feet;
how you wince as you slide out,
        stagger backwards as my spine starts to ache
        and I hold my own feet;
how you must see for a moment an open hole
        and remnants of what you left;
how I wish I could see that too;
and why have we reached the bottom of this slide,
        because I want you to go deeper,
        crush yourself into me further.

Confessional Poem, Age Seven

Uncle Dennis is the entire state of Texas,
expanse of great prairie and oil-rigged

skyscrapers all contained in the rotunda
of his five-foot-eight frame.

But when my parents bring him home
from Houston, it is 1990. My uncle

does not wear his Stetson,
does not hug me into the cowboy

flank of his new-fangled body.
Uncle Dennis is skinny, is not

Uncle Dennis until I walk beside
his wheelchair, down

the long, bleached hallway
of the nursing home, when he turns

to me, says, *Howdy, cowpoke.*
Months pass. On the playground

that is being seven years old,
I kiss my best friend Eric Schmitt

behind the dugout. He shoves me
into the dirt and runs away

as my uncle's radio moans,
If you wanna know, if he loves you so,

it's in his kiss. That's where it is.
But I am a child, one who never

learns quick. That night we visit
Uncle Dennis. When Mother whispers

into my ear, *Give your uncle a kiss
on the cheek*, the KS lesion flowers

above the neckline of his pale blue
hospital gown, a blossom that creeps

like ivy across the distance
of starched sheets between us,

into the garden, fertile, that is
my boy body, and I refuse him.

Steiner Crushes Derrida

or, Veganism for Boys

I gave up vegetarianism after seven years for a boy named Sam, who wasn't even gay. But he was tall and slender and had white hair and a baby face and he wore boots and never cleaned his bathroom. We went to dinner, and I ordered fish.

∽

Now I have returned to the fold and joined a more fundamentalist sect. Boys and what I'd rather not explain be damned.

∽

On nights I can't sleep, I watch YouTube videos. One of my three dogs curls at my feet under my desk. The other two lay on beds behind me. Lately, I've been watching videos—advertisements, blogs—about laser tattoo removal. I do not feel the need to watch these videos during the day.

∽

The tattoo on the inside of my right arm almost disappears if I put my arm palm-down on the desk. Only the stems of the "V" extend upward to remind me that, late on the night we met, I had the word "vegan" written on my body in black, vegan ink. (All my tattoos are vegan.) The difficulty of hiding such a tattoo was—is—the point. The tattoo functions as both public announcement and self-reminder. It's the adult counterpart to the Christian tattoos—the band of thorns around the upper arm or lower leg, the fish, the Bible verses—I wanted as a teenager.

∽

On my list of evasive bullshit: companion species and co-evolution; eating well; dying well; aporia, apropos decisions and responsibilities; posthumanism. On my list of evasive bullshitters: most animal studies scholars, and hipsters who make faux difficult decisions about eating meat.

∼

I have lost two dogs, the first through no fault of my own. He collapsed one day, fell over while walking from my office to the laundry room. We rushed him to the vet who told us that a tumor we never knew about had ruptured. He died, on the surgical table, of internal bleeding, his upper lip folded under itself to reveal canines we had last seen when using a corn broom to shoo him away from a rain-soaked piece of birthday cake.

I lost my second dog several years later, when I lived alone. I returned home to find that she had coughed up blood again. There was no diagnosis. What was clear was only that she sneezed blood, that she was generally lethargic and sometimes wobbly and now always incontinent. But whether she was suffering—and what suffering even meant for her—I do not know. Nor do I know whether killing her that afternoon was more about alleviating her suffering or mine.

∼

How to fight about yogurt with the one you love. 1—Assume regular grocery-shopping responsibilities. 2—Believe that animals should not be harmed for reasons of pleasure, amusement, or convenience. 3—Become a vegan based on this principle. The logic, you know, is crushing; all efforts at complication fall before it. 4—Observe that most people around you share your principle but violate it every time they sit down to eat or go shopping for clothes. 5—Refuse to buy any of the dairy products your partner still consumes.

∼

Listen to Steiner train the disciples in how to take up the cross: "Let us say that the principle or rule in question is that we ought never to use animal products for the satisfaction of our desires, and say that I sincerely embrace this principle. Does this mean that every time I chose in accordance with the principle, I am doing something purely mechanical and unthinking, and that my choices are attended by good conscience? Hardly. What it means, particularly in the living contemporary context of a society in which vegans are widely dismissed as kooks and frequently derided for being self-righteous water-walkers, is that one faces constant anguish—not simply in the sense that one suffers the mockery of one's fellow human beings, nor simply in the sense that one is acutely aware that the vast majority of other people are not following the principle and hence are perpetuating a regime of animal exploitation that arguably exceeds the magnitude of any human holocaust, but more importantly in the sense that uses of animals are so intimately interwoven into our cultural practices that pure veganism is a practical impossibility."[20]

～

"Do you regret it," a friend asks me several days after its acquisition.

The skin is starting to sting and peel, and I am impatient now to get back into the pool. I had just started to develop my butterfly. "Of course not."

But a text arrives later that afternoon telling me the tattoo is pretentious, and I say yes. And longing for water I think back to when the texter and I went swimming.

"*So hairy!*"

"I stopped shaving after we broke up."

"I never took you to be an otter."

～

Derrida's critique of human exceptionalism is crushing. Yet Derrida does not preach veganism, or even the hypocrisy of vegetarianism. He suspects principles and turns every ethical decision into a version of Abraham responding to God's call to sacrifice Isaac. But honestly, fucker, it's not that complicated. And God forbid we took the same attitude to all principles. *Thou shalt not rape.* "I am against rape in my soul," Derrida might say. And God doesn't exist. And defending Abraham or his God in any way seems monstrous, not only because a human life is almost lost, but also because a ram, caught in the thicket, loses his life instead.

∼

"Then God said, 'I give you every seed-bearing plant on the face of the whole earth and every tree that has fruit with seed in it. They will be yours for food" (Genesis 1.29).

I now have a crush on a vegan otter. He texts at 7:44 AM: "Vegan update to make up for the public mourning: morning routine is now an avocado banana kale almond milk smoothie. Good morning!"

The slide from *mourning* to *morning* makes me smile.

The public mourning in question concerns the bomb explosions at the Boston Marathon. Although our leaders warn us against misanthropy, I wonder how many people mourning the many injuries and two deaths of people they didn't know also sat down that night to dine on a corpse. I also wonder how many people died in car accidents today. Or of curable diseases. Or in other tragedies. Those lives that don't count as such or as much because they're not human, or not American. Those lives that suffered a death that has the misfortune of being routine.

I wonder too if I am being self-righteous.

I think *good morning love* as I scoop peanut butter into my oatmeal and watch Howard take his breakfast up the stairs. Howard who eats fish and eggs and cheese and drinks milk because being a vegan makes you "socially difficult," although he readily acknowledges the moral superiority of my position.

Our basset hound, Milton, does his morning yoga on the kitchen floor and turns to follow Howard.

Your next text: "I also had a dream of us: I was stripping to an acoustic cover of Pour Some Sugar on Me for you and Howard. You liked it. He didn't. And then I woke up thinking it was real."

That would be real, I think, thinking too that being a vegan is much easier when affection ameliorates an anguish that despite my deepest devotion is not constant.

At the Bathhouse, Scholars Discuss the Oceanic Feeling

A Miltonist and a Poet walk into a steamroom.
The Miltonist says, *I want to watch you fuck him*.

The Poet does not hear this because the Miltonist
does not say this. But the Poet knows this truth.

Freud says it's natural we long to see ourselves
as one with the world. That the ego has a way

of denying dangers it sees in threat of this desire.
The Poet will claim he does not want to possess

the Miltonist. A typewriter drips on his enjambed
chest as the Poet fucks a man for the Miltonist.

What these two boys know is especially this: *perhaps
everyone wants to be desired for possession*. Satan

heaves on the arm of the Miltonist as he watches
the Poet fuck. Their tattoos, a permanent possession

under the dim wattage of steamroom fluorescents.
I watch you finish and finish myself, wipe the sweat

from my eyes, the past from my feet, as we leave.

Notes

[1] Aranye Fradenburg, "Momma's Boys," *Shakesqueer: A Queer Companion to the Complete Works of Shakespeare*, ed. Madhavi Menon (Durham: Duke University Press, 2011), 319.

[2] Gilles Deleuze, "Letter to a Harsh Critic," in *Negotiations: 1972-1990*, Trans. Martin Joughin (New York: Columbia University Press, 1997), 6.

[3] Stephen Greenblatt, "Fiction and Friction," *Shakespearean Negotiations: The Circulation of Social Energy in Renaissance England* (Berkeley: University of California Press, 1988), 66-93.

[4] Michael Warner, "Tongues Untied: Memories of a Pentecostal Boyhood," *Curiouser: On the Queerness of Children*, ed. Steven Bruhm and Natasha Hurley (Minneapolis: University of Minnesota Press, 2004), 221.

[5] Jonathan Dollimore, "Towards the Paradoxical Perverse and Perverse Dynamic," in *Sexual Dissidence: Augustine to Wilde, Freud to Foucault* (Oxford: Oxford University Press, 1991), 103-30.

[6] Jonathan Goldberg, "Romeo and Juliet's Open Rs," *Queering the Renaissance* (Durham: Duke University Press, 1993).

[7] Touré, *I Would Die 4 U: Why Prince Became an Icon* (New York: Atria, 2013), 64-66.

[8] Ibid., 134.

[9] Foucault, Michel. *History of Sexuality: Volume One* (New York: Vintage, 1990), 6.

[10] Touré, *I Would Die 4 U*, 134.

[11] Lee Edelman, *No Future: Queer Theory and the Death Drive* (Durham, NC: Duke University Press, 2004), 9.

[12] José Esteban Muñoz, *Cruising Utopia: The Then and There of Queer Futurity* (New York: New York University Press, 2009), 6.

[13] Oscar Wilde, *The Picture of Dorian Gray,* ed. Michael Patrick Gillespie (New York: W.W. Norton, 2006), 3.

[14] Wayne Koestenbaum, *Cleavage: Essays on Sex, Stars, and Aesthetics* (New York: Ballantine Books, 2000), 7.

[15] *Instructions for American Servicemen* (1942 reprt; Oxford: Oxford University Press, 2004).

[16] Ibid., 17.

[17] Koestenbaum, *Cleavage*, 17.

[18] Sigmund Freud, *Three Essays on the Theory of Sexuality*, trans. James Stratchey (New York: Basic Books, 1962), 52.

[19] Eve Sedgwick, "White Glasses," *Tendencies.* (Durham, NC: Duke University Press, 1993), 257.

[20] Gary Steiner, *Animals and the Limits of Postmodernism* (New York: Columbia University Press, 2013), 63.

Acknowledgments

Thank you to the editors of the following publications, where sometimes slightly different versions of some of these pieces previously appeared: *Assaurcus, Animal, Avidly, Big Lucks, Connotation Press, Folio, The Indiana Review, LAMBDA Literary Review, Moon City Review, PANK,* and *Weave.*

"Sonnet before Introduction to Shakespeare" originally appeared in *This Assignment is So Gay: LGBTIQ Poets on the Art of Teaching,* from Sibling Rivalry Press.

Will Stockton would like to thank Jesus, obvi. And Howard, who is like Jesus but more merciful.

D. Gilson thanks Robert McRuer and Holly Dugan, his queer parents; the cohort of queers who have welcomed him at The George Washington University; and Jessica Server, his sister wife.

Thanks, too, to Jeffrey Jerome Cohen for hooking us up; Eileen Joy and Kam Aghtan for pouncing on the project with crushing enthusiasm; Caleb Suttles for indulging our narcissistic desire for self-portraits; and Bryan Borland and Seth Pennington for publishing *Crush*'s queer-sibling chapbook *Gay Boys Write Straight Porn* (Sibling Rivalry Press).

This book is dedicated to all the boys—past, present, and future—on whom we crush.

5761171R00068

Printed in Great Britain
by Amazon.co.uk, Ltd.,
Marston Gate.